ISBN: 9798685695055

With Love

HELLO, NORMAL.
WHERE HAVE YOU BEEN?

Brian d'Entremont

It was early this year,
a day long ago,
most everything normal
left town on the go.

A return to the regular,
the standard routine,
the things we all love,
what a wonderful scene!

A place so familiar,
our everyday sound.
So long to that world;
it's been tossed, spun around.

On its return,
we'll sing and dance 'round.
Scream with excitement,
feet running the ground.

Until that day comes,
we'll practice in place.
Prepare for our normal
with patience and grace.

So on to that question,
what you came here to learn;
why is this happening?
When will normal return?

They call it corona
and COVID-19.

Or simply the germies,
is what those words mean.

Keep washing your hands.

Put on a mask.

Stay a safe distance,

our everyday task.

Elbows, no hugs.

Class on a screen.

Sports in the yard.

aygrounds go unseen.

And the worst part of all,
we miss all our friends.
Our grandparents, our cousins;
the list never ends.

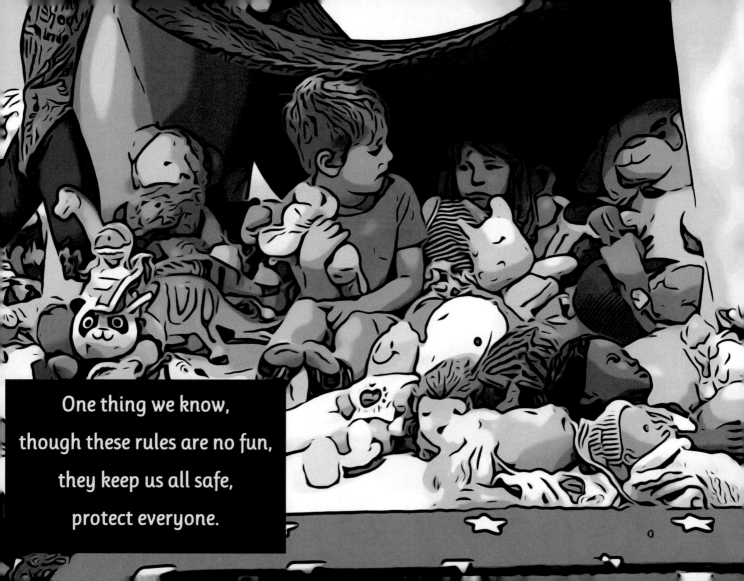

One thing we know,
though these rules are no fun,
they keep us all safe,
protect everyone.

Now this part is tricky:
the question of when,
we'll welcome home normal,
ask where it has been.

Doctors, nurses, and scientists,
all the world's best,
are working to fix this;
it's their mission, their quest.

In the meantime we'll play,
we'll make our own joy.
Oh, the things that we'll do,
the ideas we'll deploy.

We'll make art out of everything.

Slide down the stairs.

Epic games in the yard.

Forts constructed from chairs.

We'll do this thing and that,
find games everywhere.
Some new things, some weird things,
that thing over there.

Watch TV like kings,
so much more than before.
Movie nights are a standard,
treats and popcorn galore.

Alongside each other,
with family that's near.
More time together,
more laughter to hear.

So when normal returns,
we'll be arms-open-wide.
Say, "We're doing okay...
now come on inside!"

THE END

Thank you to the
healthcare workers, scientists, first responders, and essential workers
who are fighting the COVID-19 battle.

Made in the USA
Middletown, DE
22 September 2020